Mouth Sugar & Smoke

Eric Tran

Diode Editions
PO Box 5585
Richmond, Virginia 23220-0585
www.diodeeditions.com

Diode Editions is an independent press based in Doha, Qatar and Richmond, Virginia.
Patty Paine founded the press in 2012 as an offshoot of *Diode Poetry Journal*.

Our mission is to beautifully craft our books, and to fanatically support our authors.

Patty Paine, Founding Editor-in-Chief
Law Alsobrook, Art Director & Editor
Zoë Shankle Donald, Managing Editor
Cover illustration *Apollo and Hyacinthus* by Mazahir Hussain
Author photo courtesy of Emily Herschl

Table of Contents

Aubade with Withdrawal

Somehow I've slept under the buzzing
sun of the detox center lobby.

When I wake, you're gone
behind the locked doors. I had almost—

what's the word, expected? hoped?
—for a short goodbye, like a punch

on the shoulder, your lips
letting some tiny breath turn

into song. The attendants see me
startle awake and play polite,

like they're too familiar
with this loss. *What do you know*

about me, I want to ask. Not
from anger, truly, but because time

is always a question.
                    When night slips

its sequined dress
                    back on, it's still night

so sure of the perfect
                    time to leave

and in its wake
                    a ripple hiding

blackbirds, brackish
                    silt with hundreds

of eyes
        looking in all directions.

Poem Starting with Underwear and Ending with Ghost

On my last week of wards, when hospital work has become so routine I could ghost in and out emergencies in minutes if needed, I bring a 2-pack of y-fronts. I tried to picture the heft of my patient while at the dollar store. I know so much that he has yet to tell me: how many bottles of Tylenol he knocked back, to start. He begins his days with a case of Pabst in the morning and finishes before dinner. His husband of a quarter decade died a month ago. He didn't arrange for someone to feed his mini schnauzer because the near dead don't make plans. He may know I signed the order that stops him from going home to feed the schnauzer, but there's a doorway between knowing and remembering. Today he's washing his single pair of underpants in the sink as there's no one to bring him more— near dead, plans. He won't know I left the briefs with his nurse. He doesn't know in the last year one of my friends died, one friend overdosed, one died of overdose. The near dead I know, the dead I know near me. This week I'm too sad to go home right after work, but I—arrogantly—have only planned time for the known dead. I know, plans: the first step towards failure. My dead don't remember me, I know. This near dead man won't either. No one knows what ghost they leave behind.

Intervention

          I'm asked to keep
a secret and I do
          until I don't. Until he trusts

me to ration out his pills
          and I forget, so fever
holds him as I do

          a lover who moves
to leave. Until
          I oversleep so his dog

shits the carpet. Until
          I give promises
like they're bullets

          and my mouth sits
blank and hot.
          Until even the golden

pothos wilts and needs
          to be junked.
And as do the blackened

          spoons I polish
back clean and line
          up so there's an army

of my face in their bellies,
          until I see each distortion
asking for help.

Forensics Lab

University of North Carolina School of Medicine

At the coroner's they go easy,
only show us deaths
by OD. No wounds
we can see. They insist
we hydrate because our machine
bodies buckle at the knees.
The coroner's assistant
lays out her knives
like paint brushes and says
leave if we get hot at the neck.
　　　Already I'm elsewhere
when she assures us
dead bodies won't bleed
as bad as ones with hearts
that still stampede —
　　　your living room, where the cat
　　　hides in empty beer cases,
　　　sheets so sweat-soaked
　　　they're too intimate to change.
　　　The night too intimate
　　　to disturb with what I want.
And the body gives in easily
to the blade. I half
want a yelp, one of us
to go woozy to prove something's
not right. Maybe it's me who needs
to flinch. *Leave if you need*
she said
　　　but who would watch you
　　　dead-eyeing the TV?
　　　Who would witness you
　　　alive enough to blink?

The First Man I Loved Who Wasn't My Father

My college roommate, his closet full
of Abercrombie, a pillow top of loose
curls shaking as he puked in his bed.

An hour before, his drunk friends
returned him without
instruction. What did I know

to do but leave the door open,
practice my chemistry and calculus
like being good might keep anyone

alive. A lesson in love
as vigilance, as hesitation
between breath. A smart boy

sees himself in a fog
-drunk mirror. Does he open
the wound like a door

between bedrooms? One day a man
I love will ask me to stay
through the withdrawal,

then demand I leave so he can satisfy
another craving. A mouth
is of course an escape

and so two will double the exits.
Bounty. I resent no one
the instinct to run. My first love's

friends returned after not to see
if he was OK but to apologize to me.
He and I don't keep in touch.

When he moved out I cried
like an overdue raincloud,
bloodletting a bruise on the sky.

My Father Worries War is Coming

I tell him I'm dating a man
and he says if I'm so lonely
he'd drive across the country
to live with me.
He reminds me I am
his only son. He is one
of seven and half his family
died in the war. We found
his sister's photo in a temple
and the monk wouldn't let us
take it with us. My dad
never said he regretted leaving
her again, but as his son, I should
have made a home for her
      in my pocket.
Would she be lonely
next to photos of my dad
at my age? The men I've loved
have never seen those pictures.
One man said he wished he knew me
better. What is loneliness? Perfectly
strained tea. Briefly waking with
sunlight. I feel it must be quiet.
Besides himself, my father
has never seen a photo of me
      with a man I love.
What is loneliness?
Sometimes I think I'm sad
simply because I acknowledge
the world. I'm so grateful. Am I
lying if I never say this aloud?

Trust Metaphor

He gave me his box of pills
        to taper out and I held it

        in my hands like a bird
with a broken wing. No,

like a trusty, neglected
        rag tossed in my trunk, or

        a favorite resentment
I could revisit day

after day. A worry
        stone, a paper cut

        on my fingers' webbing.
The squeaky step

to his apartment
        for each morning's

        sacrament. What faith,
even when I forgot his dose

he'd say *it's OK* through
        his fever's tremble. He knew

        I'd be back. And better. A ballerina
twisting in a music box.

Detox

I scrub the burn
        from the bellies
of your spoons,
        wonder if I should just toss
them out completely
        while you watch
Game of Thrones.
        I hate how little lives
matter in this show.
        Who washes the blades
pulled from dead men's
        necks like tulips
bloomed out a magician's
        sleeve? Sometimes
there's not a new character
        to love instead. I'm afraid
enough to kneel
        and shovel your cat's
litter. Scent cloud
        of rotten OJ. Used
needles like a fist
        of Pixy Stix.
But look—it can all
        be cleaned again.
On screen a baby
        is killed. I'm thankful
you wince here.
        Raindrop of relief: if
you gasp, you're breathing.

Tops

My first one washed my hair and whispered he wanted
to dom me

in the aisles of Target. He bought me a drive-
thru dinner and offered me

one of his own shirts after
his cat shit on my polo. Friends,

I went home wearing feces.
My tenth was the first to make me feel more

than sausage
sausage casing or a boil awaiting the lance.

Is this a poem
that celebrates a man's restraint

or my freedom to feel joy?
In my first favorite tongue

my love can mean *to eat,* depending
on how I open my throat. O my soft

-edged mouth, *to love*
the shortest word you know. My last top

couldn't finish
but asked me to stay the night.

We exhausted each other
searching for comfort in the dark

Holiday Inn that smelled
like artisanal barbeque leftovers

he tried to give me
the next day. He asked how I slept.

            Wonderfully, not restfully,
beautifully, or even easily. I meant

                    just that: full
of wonder as an early morning.

                    As I drove home, the sky
flushed pink like a fist unfolding.

Bottoms

My first was so pale he
(be)came moonlight.

In fluorescence, my last
lined me up like a bullseye.

I bought one a milkshake after,
pointed at the cream-glut straw

—*you*. Call me dirty
spoon hoarder, pot-licker,

convert of the salt rim.
How my meat teeth

mark Ley lines, the soft,
plump folds in an origami box.

How breath can balloon
and moisten the edges

for tearing. My tongue wants
less violence—not *tearing*,

but like bread's warm open face
or my fingers deep in the ready.

By sweat I mean a glass
on the nightstand, my thirsty

palm on a wet-kissed
mirror. I trace

a message, a nothing
that disappears by morning

until I bring my mouth close
and watch it come to life.

Pre-Coda

Pre-cum/precaution: paint

      me precise, persuade me

prostrate, permissive

      but precarious, palpate

us pearlescent, practice

      us connected, convoluted,

piled countless positions:

      precordia colliding,

combining, a persistent

      pursuit, protracted,

patient pulsing,

      a permission,

a climbing closer

      please closer —

If Asked

Because stricture and scripture, because a man said ejaculating paused
his prostate pain, but he was still a right Catholic otherwise. Because
circumcision and circumstance, because slipping the skin can kill the
right kind of hemophilic. Because death is a test result. Because we
always check left vs. right before surgery. Because there are a lot of
organs the size of your fist. Because an impending sense of doom follows
both hemolysis and anxiety. Because my attending says he wakes to
take care of the dying and by evening remembers why he goes home
to his wife and kids. Because daily can mean night or day. Because the
intern says, *I really don't think hospitals are a place of healing.* Because ice
burns, because chiaroscuro, because you knock while you open the door.
Because metaphysics and metastasis, because pheo and pheno. Because
a murder of crows, maybe blackbird or shadow. Because frankly hospice
and hospital. Because how else do I describe my 9-year-old patient
with absence seizures when every minute is the wrong one to say she's
beautiful? Who do I tell about her staring spells—her eyes wide as if taking
in the entire world and what she sees is why she is silent, why her whole
body is shaking.

Penumbra Aubade

Here, shadeling. Come

shadow sky. Show

your borders beginning

to lose their shape.

Show me nothing

beneath those layers

but more sulcus

to plumb,

more circling

the unrisen sun.

Come quiet

tundra, come drowsy

starscape. Darken

my doorway. Time

to blanket us over.

Frequent Utilizer Protocol

Second-season wild
-flower or -fire left

to burn free, discourage
further scarring. Sensible

like weighted dice,
reliable as a scab,

as watercolor wash.
The moon bit

to the quick. Hands
empty and closed

in prayer. How to say
hello without breaking

stride. To hold water
with your teeth and still

breathe. Who misses
you? Surely, you survive

for someone. I hope
you wake as lodestar. A key

depends on the missing teeth.
A ring for every swollen

finger. A knife that hones
on meat and bone.

Ouroboros

When I decide to leave, I return
        to locking the door each night.
The lock and I agree: nothing

                gets in unless it's clever
        enough to knock. No more
           hallelujah until we pay for it,

until the recycling gets emptied.
        I bought a syringe disposal box
and to take it back, they wanted

                my name and address,
        my wallet lighter a month
           of groceries. What a joke

when we deny a problem
        sleeps in the bed.
The world spins itself

                round and full
        of fire. We're blessed
           with two full moons this month

and we have given them
        different names. Like an eye
with burst veins

                and one blue with pus
        aren't both blind. Why walk around
           the lake? You know how to swim.

Call the Mouth

Shotgun sun-
catcher honey
suckle root
water whistle
blower hard
part wishing
well oil
slick whip
stitch blister
pack rabbit
trap chapter
book candy
stash

Catapres

Did tremble at the lip
of the bottle. Tumbled

through a mouth's wide
and broken door. Flattened

myself, flattered myself
as false as any god

gone wet with prayer.
Drunk with need. Fecund

yet flaccid. Fantastic.
Mastered that first

sloppy wobble towards
you dry. Alive

at least for now. And what
nowness, what practice,

what capsule of ease.
Did breathe then, didn't we?

Vistaril

Like breath's face beat hot   with rouge
my evening   gut sucked

to kiss my spine   your name caught
in my teeth   your other name

starched with pre-cum   and still more
shaken with ice   each shard vital

and replaced and missed   to suggest
is to live   in the space before

threat   that a space away
from imagining   the empty body

of a pretty paper   finger trap
how light gives   a shadow eyes

my body remembers   river
and winter   my mind shivers

Baclofen

shiver a body's verb
your body's curse
words in my mouth
want down right

to my marrow
oh mercy me
mercury boiled
from base and bulb

like seed blown
into my hand
on yours on a knob
cranked in circles

hurry holy how
the body can't wait

Bentyl

What a body weighs when it wants.
Swell, we say. How *full* slants

to *fool*. How a body empties
and still sings like a drum

or a teething beast.
At our core, we want

a day free of wanting.
I know I demanded your bitterness

splashed across my tongue.
Finger beds white

and wet, desperate
for aftermath. To cum

is to grip upon
relief. Unload me

like a gun. Make the sky
crack with lightning.

Naloxone

Again, lightning
bug. Stiletto breath,
sing the shotgun

of an engine starting.
Tiptoe the ledge,
a body suspended

in sleep. Poppy gone
to seed, burnt under
summer's unforgiving

affection. Brutal
and begging. Braggart,
belabored.

Deepest nightshade,
ripen on the vine.

Motivational Interviewing

Me flushed ripe as a zit.
Like chafe between the thighs,

a pair of prettied lips.
Mercy like milk in the mouth,

on the fire my tongue
woke with flicker. Yes, sir,

I'd like to know butter
draped down my throat.

Like men drowned in honey,
sweet meat made into cure.

Give me golden skin, tight
and swollen as a flooded river.

Your hand on my chest, my bloat.
Give my mouth that sugar and smoke.

Papaver Somniferum

Smoke in the kitchen. Impatience
choking up the bedroom, sweat
slicked down the elbow's crook.

Once you flooded my sink
with empties, with defrost,
spoons that fed me honey

and you something sweeter.
What is the world if not for wanting?
I admit I've wanted your picked-at

scab, your broken voice through a
morning-night call. Bran flakes just hours
later. And what I want now is a sliver

caught between my teeth. Butter and bite.
Fire in my mouth. A whole field alight.

Suboxone

Fire eater, field seeder.
Who saw thirst so wept a storm,

saw dirt so made a home.
Dried to bone then coaxed

back to sob and wet,
led back to morning

song. The voice cracked
to let the light get in.

Through the throat's strained
glass, some flowers

grow nearly wild. A measure
of freedom. Maybe a disguise,

a surprise. Let the mouth
hold it tight as a secret.

Tramadol

I wanted to hold
secrets as a bruise
holds blood, holds

memory of teeth
and mouth deep as
a lake. Close

as a shadow
boxer's fingers
clenched into

a rose. Isn't
that us — close
as the punch

and its recoil. Thud
as heavy as sleep.

Enmesh

I never rode in your car because we each valued control. I kept my hand on the wheel, you kept me out. Chiaroscuro: how negative space defines the space. How, even then, the binary fails us. Like a promise does. Like there can be your body and not your body. Your body and my body. Like an echo isn't the sound and its own sound. A dream, I learn, can process the waking. When I go to bed I'm already thinking of morning. I unlace my favorite shoes, point them at door. Shake out my virgin wool sweater. Another animal's hide I will wear as a mantle.

Lexapro

Some nights the last bottles / left full / on the mantle. / Your eyes orbit another / blockbuster thick with bloodied / extras. When the nerves die / in our noses / we'll drown / our plates in salt and acid so at least / the tongue remembers / fullness. / In medical school, I learned not to fear / how much someone uses / but how much they use and still feel nothing. / How depression is tolerance to hopelessness. / Like a body / -sized dent in the bed makes / an invitation to return. / How rest resembles / collision. / Some nights you sleep / and I leave / on all the lights / in my deer brain. Of course, berries need / to be gnashed before growing buds / from their graves. / Of course, we forgive / flesh for its sweetness. / Aftertaste itself an absence. / A memory. Drugs are measured / in half-lives. / I've learned the other half isn't empty, but full of emptiness.

Zofran

Your mouth empty as a church,
soft and seeded, sour like sun
-ripe citrus. Once I believed
I could swallow the bitter
pits and gestate a whole fruit tree.
There's something (*a seed*) unsettling
about how sexy a thought
this is, like how at first the weight
loss dug deeper valleys around
the peaks of your biceps. A moan
of surrender cuts night the same
as one that echoes in the toilet bowl.
In a draft, I replaced *seed* with *need*.
A joke that turned into a question.

Trazodone

We turned as a lock. Like tender
for a debtor but hotter

than a rash. Guzzled
down a storm

drain. We danced some
nights: if you called

I jumped like a stone
atop the water. Broke

as a bird and its song.
Morning a bargain

we made as if wealthy
or desperate. Gullible,

like lovers, to solve
a crisis with light.

Nocturne

You call at crisis hour,
crevice between crying

and quiet hours, to say I'm stupid
to ask if you're safe. My stupid

heartbeat like it could keep us
both alive. Stupid bed of vessels.

Stupid sweat-soaked sheets,
extra stash in the box spring.

Stupid night, slow
on its splinted leg.

Stupid sleepless
son of a bitch—swears

at the suffering as hot
and clean as a pistol's mouth.

Burnout

My lips around a pistol
like petals. Beat —

how the sun on your body
is also a kiss. How wanting

enough spins shock
into flushing. One burns

to ghost, the other an impatient
mouth. How dirt starved for seed

holds a grave warm and welcome
as a bed for another man

to leave stains and flower.
My tongue will empty itself

of demands, burn tender
into time. Sugar into smoke.

Commuting by the Confederate Flag on I-40

flown half-mast. I want
to write about the suffocating

enormity, but against
the sky's slick skin, it dangles

like a tired bandage.
I don't want to forgive

so easily. I want
to play the angry faggot

but in truth I burn
to know what grief

demotes your pride,
neighbor. Did you lose

your son, a lover,
a dog? Does it matter

my best friend died,
and he was gay?

One of the last things
he said was, *Be nice*

to me, I don't feel well.
I mean to say we're all

so small. I'm scared
for any of us

to run out of gas
in an unfamiliar place.

Remember? Coasting
slow, an action

so gentle you forget
to breathe.

Starting with a Line by Frank Ocean
Interviewing Timothee Chalamet

Almost like this quiet search for joy.
This hyacinth bulb in winter

with promise of carmine, blood
cupped fresh from the heart.

River broad belly right up
to the rock bed's lip. Pressed

close to bruise, which you know
blooms without protest

if you ask just right. Like the face
of a puddle accepting new

drops of rain. Falling can be
lying down if there's no fight

in the descent.

Scenes

How's a man
  give another

a nickname? Black
  and brackish

night. I don't cry
  but I would

watch myself
  drown in

bruises.
  How's a man

knock another
  down just to watch

him stand
  back up?

   ❋

Am I a faggot
  of kindling

or a tiny bird,
  wings outstretched

in the dirt,
  the downshot

gaze, cherished
  breath between

notes of song
  or sobbing.

✳

We meet in
my night black
heart, a mouth
full of rain
and concrete.
Under shadow
we pretend
rich as black-
birds, we collide
or collapse.
How the ocean
touches sand.

Great Pretender

French kissin' lizard lips
      Gloss-slick thick to ease

            a heat beaten engine
      Bouquet of toothache

plant fist of dirt
      grown Novocain

            Bleached out bottle
neck Sterile shattered

sugared So thin
      almost nothing

            how light breaks
along its spine

to grow longer
      shadows A man I loved

            remembered favorite meals
but not the joy

of fat relaxed
      on his tongue

            How he couldn't sleep
naked beside me

How's liquor open
      a jammed-up door Drunk

            shepherd remind me
how the sun sets

across the snake's back
      Remember dark

            water fish make their own
version of light

My Father Worries War is Coming

He practiced nonviolence
outside the home. I may doubt
the purpose of the back of a hand

now, but he worked as a mechanic
and took a wire brush to the soft
palms that held night dark.

Sundays he tucked slicks
of soy sauce into scrambled eggs,
still the softest I remember. How

electric I felt when he brought
two fists to my face   *listen*
and the song of caught

crickets. How could they know
who was listening? Why I insist
on clapping soft. I'm grateful

I've made my own calluses,
but my skin can promise

integrity and still break.
I'm surprised   *delighted?*
to remember blood runs

hot when it wants to run.
Listen, no hand keeps all
the light out. Winter

touches every branch.
What can we want? Now. To be
held as the body holds breath.

Portraits of Handwashing

after Bernard Cooper

I.

Soap the backs of your hands, too. You are a pinwheel of contact points; more than your palms have touched the world today. Flood the fine creases of your wrists, bury the mountains of your knuckles. Each finger is a molting snake, each hand an unbaptized infant. Look: Your forearms end in clouds. The sink is a fresh-made bed, and your hands carry so many weary travelers.

II.

Lasse, my dorm's health educator, taught us to lather for at least two rounds of "Happy Birthday." He had a lingering Swedish accent and unironically loved the Swedish fish gummies I bought him for Christmas. *Happy birthday to you!* he sang. He sang so happily we felt like it was actually all our birthdays; his mimed lathering was our puppet show. When Lasse caressed my fevered forehead, I imagined him later, at the sink, humming himself bright and clean again.

III.

A nurse visited our class and implored us to be vigilant: *When you enter a patient's room, when you leave.* She wanted to say, *You could save lives,* but she actually said, *You could kill people.* She waved her arms emphatically, flapped like them a bird in distress, or maybe she was just air-drying her hands. Maybe she had just washed them. Maybe her hands, which looked thick and strong even from seven rows back, had just held a pink, wailing newborn or palmed a syringe of adrenaline for another patient's stilled heart.

IV.

In New York, I know three bakers who wash their hands, their counters, their instruments before spinning together white sugar flowers. In North Carolina, my neighbor scoops lumps out of a litter box. Elsewhere, after a potter presses out a wide-mouthed bowl, a 5-year-old picks his nose. A butcher, a barehanded fisherman. Somewhere, someone on a great first date uses the bathroom and lingers in the mirror. Mouths to his hands, *Oh my god. Oh my god.*

V.

Once, as a kid, I tried to make a kite out of chopsticks and printer paper, but it never caught air. When my dad got home from the mechanic shop, he sighed at my attempt. With a small grout brush, he scrubbed the oil from his hands before building me a new one. Once, he cupped a family of crickets and held them near my ear. Once, he slapped me down to kitchen tile and then iced my bruise. His kite flew above our apartment rooftop. He wanted me to hold the string, but I refused, afraid it might slip, even from a tightly clenched fist.

The First X-Ray

Wilhem Roentgen aimed radiation at his test subjects,
each holding photons like a dam holds flood.
What spilled over was cast on film, a portrait

of what was lost: a metal sheet, a set of weights,
his wife's hand — silhouette of her wedding ring.
The history of innovation cycles, a stone wheel

that hones a knife's edge. Biotech is built small
for warzones, to trace poison in water. Mustard gas
fathered chemo: autopsies of blistered victims

showed tumors lulled into slumber. Wildfires
clear stagnant fields nude and eventually you
hardly remember the earth's scarred flesh. Still,

I remember cadavers and my reluctant scalpel
baring down onto bone. I remember someone
said, *They wanted you to learn*, as if permission

could supplant the image of skin peeled out
like an onion. Roentgen saw this muddled
future; he called them X-rays, *x* for unknown,

but he predicted deformed fingers, twisted bowels,
and hid behind lead. Even his wife, mother
of lobar pneumonia, of excised bullets and clots,

knew her role in this play. At her naked
knuckles, she cried, *I have seen my death*,
but not once did she pull her hand away.

My dearest resident Brian,

my assigned a med student at 6AM Brian, my Florsheims pounding the linoleum because this morning's patients are especially sick Brian, my muttering to himself about urine outputs and losartan dosages in the hallway Brian (but lilted voice around patients, *sorry to hear you didn't sleep well* Brian), my worries about Mr. Donaldson's 30-pack-year smoking habit, my calling for the X-ray reading of a lung nodule Brian, my up late writing notes Brian, my still finds time for giving advice about clinical rotations Brian, my *the only feedback so far is to lose the tie* Brian, my *I only survived med school because of my wife* Brian, my Brian with multiple pagers that you won't give to another intern because they had it last night, my still thinking about Mrs. Rodriguez's heart attack in room 33 Brian, my *I'm not scared I'll get in trouble, I'm scared she'll be hurt*, my I've never seen you take lunch so I bring you two donuts in the AM Brian, my *this day is my picture of disaster* but keeps walking towards the next room and smiles Brian, my when did your skin see sun last Brian, my does each day collapse into the next Brian, my I hope you slept some hours last night Brian, my please hydrate Brian, my we've got news Brian, my when you finally took a break Brian, my we got the results Brian, my it's not cancer Brian, my did you hear us Brian, my wild fires can burn eucalyptus trees black and charred Brian, my but they grow back at the tree tops not at the base Brian, my did you hear us Brian, my survival is seen both in the wreckage and away from it Brian, my it's not cancer Brian, my sometimes it's not cancer, Brian, some days it's not cancer

Untitled (Portrait of Ross in L.A.):
Mixed Material: Felix Gozalez-Torres: 1991

Because lately all joints seem rustle twist; rising from reclining hospital beds, from cabs and laps, some human part spills off the edges. On the worst days, the body anagrams spleen and sulcus, shine and surface. On the worst days, the body props and leans in those final selfies. The world swarms with hands — clumsy, numbed grasping for blood and breath and breast. And really no God-blessed matter can be touched and remain. No fire, no burnished doorknob. No senile woman whose head I hold still for central line placement. Not her heart's pace when we move too slow. Not her ribs snapped clean in CPR. Not your hand or mine, enclosed as the covers of a book. But if my body was dust, was subway stubs and footprints and we piled it up, would we call it healed? New or novel? I'm asking you to take your palms and push — tonight, make me whole again.

10 Responses to a Clickbait Headline

Australian Man Wakes From Coma Speaking Fluent Mandarin
Proving Again the Brain is a Wondrous Thing—IJReview.com

A stroke survivor makes his living touring schools with the story of his recovery. He told me he remembers nouns the best; for the abstract he thought in rhymes: for this and there, he pictured kiss and bear, maybe *piss* and *hair*, *mist* and *snare*.

Sometimes the brain is the weakest link, the first chain to snap under duress. Insomnia, UTI, too few leafy greens can erase all the names in your family, make you think the neighbor is being kidnapped, force you to wonder, *Is this room filled with cats real or imagined?*

My friend says that when on molly, whomever you're with becomes family. *But it's all real,* she insisted, *you're still close when you're sober again.* In high school, they told us MDMA burned holes in your brain, Swiss cheese in your skull. New studies show it still may cause neurodamage, but may also treat PTSD, may delete neurons but maybe the ones that hold onto violence, reflexes for balling your hands into fists.

I've stopped watching TV shows with violence, where characters are slammed against walls, knocked unconscious to remove them from fight scenes. I flinch each time, wondering how many concussions a person can get before they left the scene permanently.

In sundowning, patients who depend on the sun to right themselves get confused by lengthening shadows, begin to shake and pace aimlessly, as if there isn't enough light to remind them how to put one foot in front of the other.

Imagine finding your son awake from a coma, returned after months of silence. Would you cry that he talked again, or that you didn't know what he meant by *jia*, home, or *jia ting*, family?

Alien hand syndrome can occur after surgery to cure epilepsy. The hand can feel foreign, autonomous. It can be bratty and push away a chair you mean to pull close or naughty and creep up your thigh while you sleep. Some patients give this hand a name and when it throws away their microwave burrito say, *Oh Henry doesn't like it when I don't eat well.*

A neuro professor once told me that time moves faster as you age because kids pack boxes with their toys spilling out the top and adults fold and tuck into suitcases. The brain learns how to speed towards those last few days.

I spend a lot of time in my head thinking of synonyms, slant-definitions, things that slip around the edges. For *wondrous*, maybe *miraculous* like God, *staggering* like one drink too many. *Precious* like crystal glasses, *sublime* like looking from a mountaintop—unsure how deep the valley is below.

I once worked in a hospice where a husband moved in with his dying wife. He told me sometimes he stayed awake with his finger under her nose to know she was breathing. He was developing dementia himself, told me: *I just couldn't live without my wife, I mean son, no I mean my wife. My wife.*

Hell of a Time

The sky a moth
-eaten curtain. Or dusty

table, the moon a broken
water ring, a mess

of sugar hastily
wiped up. Accident, proof

we were here, not quite
touching how we want

to caress the face
of a fresh-sprung flower

or knuckle through
barely-there ice. Season

of dying
dandelions,

see how we can allow
life to breathe

if we just wait.
Hello, papercut

on my lover's lips,
hello peach

branch broken
into bloom. Soon,

though until then, good
morning—this one

and the next and the next
and

Ode to Bossy Bottoms

Marvel, popped up
        like tulips in snow.
                Urgent bell
        in a boxing ring,
sharp as the lip
        of a rocks glass. Music
                box of baubles
        that bites me back.
Lit, uncracked
        coil, tin pan
                batter boiling over.
        Hello, sour cherry center
-fold. Good night,
        miracle text, book
                on my lap,
        pressed with petals
or names run
        wet with a single
                hot finger.

Cadaver Lab

I figured it'd be months without laughter.
Understandably. On pelvic dissection day
my friend Amelia whispers, *I'm sorry,*

girlfriend before starting the saw.
Another friend unknowingly holds

his cadaver's hand during the biggest
incisions. Classmates I don't even like
point out veins and nerves to spare me

hours of inhaling fat and fascia. Then
one group finds a penis pump and we decide

yes, he meant it as a surprise and the boys
fist-bump his cold hands. Another group
shares their cadaver's perfect pink polish,

another has fresh, unwrinkled ink
across her chest. Like tiny treasures

for us. Of course, the body is a gift.
Of course, no one donates their body
without a sense of humor. On dissection days

we all leave hungry, specifically for chicken.
I book my calendar with hook-ups

as if to practice how blood flows
while it can. One boy I bring home
has a scar down his sternum, a souvenir

of a heart condition. He apologizes
years after the incision healed, like the scar

wasn't a lovely pink. I imagine the lights
baring down on him, how so many lucky
hands got to press against his skin.

Scenes

does he speak / does he break

a fever / when you undress

the door / of his throat

as certain / as rain held

in both hands / of drought

like petals / made silk

in the body / of a book

does he swallow / silence

like blood / dark wine

No dark, just lush, the fullest
green and braided leather. Teeth

and throat bare. Incisor and instep.
Two fists of crushed brocade

under your back. Swollen door,
fitted, heavy wood. Careless

window without a shutter.
The china tree in midnight:

arms full of leaves
bitten into stars.

It's easier, my blood
outside me   Hotter

under sunlight   Held
in a chipped teacup or between

your thighs   I could take
us for roses this way

I could tender my hand
and see jam on your lips

✳

I'd unshell you in the sun,
spill you on the hot baked brick.

Stained white with ready. Emptied,
right there in God's open garden.

A bed from every swell of dirt,
plow each two knuckles deep

and two more wide. Make soft
the roots and stems. Tremble

the boughs naked of leaves.
Let the ground grow wet with fruit.

Double Depression

I learn it means people prone to sadness
who develop depression, but it reminds me

of a favorite Chinese restaurant: Double
Happiness, where they snuck me extra

fortune cookies for my loyalty,
or a double rainbow, that oversaturated

miracle. What's that they say about
the necessity of rain? I'm sorry, double

depressed, I don't mean to make light
of your sorrow, I mean only to say

I love you as I look into the two-sided
mirror and see you and then myself,

as a set of bunk beds for adults,
how the heart has two of each

chamber, which fill and collapse
in unison, as song underneath another song.

Explaining Psychiatry to My ESL Relatives

Spelled like hairstylist,
only *under* the scalp.
Sounds like scotch tape
across a punctured
tire. Circumference
of a spider's egg
hidden in chocolate.
Sing iambic,
sign Iago and chasm,
just don't say
psychic. Semantics,
but words matter
to us. We're pious
and subversive,
or try to be
clean as a punch
struck straight
as a shoreline,
like a poem
ending with symbol
of a tree.

On the Psychotic Unit

My patient calls everything crazy but herself. The pattern of mandalas in a coloring book we work through together, some sudden yelling in the hall, last bits of blonde surviving at the tips of my hair. In respect, I swore off this word, its cousins and papier-mâché masks.

I also swore not to write about patients when it's not mostly about me, but here I am, ushering patients into the library during a fire alarm. My patient says it's crazy when I close the unbreakable, suffocating door, how I've trapped them like matchsticks.

Another patient spat in my face and maybe if I squinted I could imagine he saw a snap of flame. How the fire is stopped by making a wish. How to remember joy.

After the fire, my patient is visited by her estranged son, who brings flowers he must take home with him. They matched the pink lipstick she hasn't mustered the energy to wear. *It's crazy*, she says after. *This whole thing made my day.*

How My Mother Named Me

She forgets English words. To her, I live
in *North Coraline*, even when I leave her
my address on a Post-it. She forgot
the baby name book in the lobby,
because when you're screaming
the name of a goddess you left
overseas, you'll forget names
of other folks' kids. She settled
on Eric—eternal, ruler,
destroyer. She hates the name
but it's fast and easy to write
on form after form after form
you don't understand. Credit to her
I could have been named *ultrasound*
or *sterile*, or *gook* or *chink*
or *dragon lady*. I imagine
she heard that like a mosquito
bite you've scratched into scar.
She wishes she had named me better
in a language we no longer share.
Expensive dragon, she translates, but no,
not when six aunts shared a bedroom
right before my birth. *Golden*,
like what they traded smugglers
for safety, what they didn't have
for food in the camps. Not that
either. I would give you more examples
of what keeps us apart, my soft
hands, but she keeps from me
those memories. *Precious.*
That's it. Precious dragon.

Apology to My Beloved

after Jessica Jacobs

Whose winter blooms surprise me: crocus
and iris and daffodil. Then come limp-tongue lilies,

bleeding heart, and, dear God, the love in the mist.
Who named these plants and can you question
why I used to hate flowers. How I was convinced

to resent such schmaltz and ease.
Yesterday, I watched a man run out the shitty Ingles

(*Shingles* we say in this part of town)
right into stalled traffic, cradling neon mums.
Imagine, flowers where you buy your meat

and TP, a version of me says. Another refuses
to believe you can buy your happiness or your way

out of anxiety. He says you'll piss out
the vitamins, grow nose blind to the scent-thick candle,
and worry how long 'til the petals give it up

to gravity. I'm sorry how this man loves you.
In high school, my boyfriend rarely held my hand

in public, lied about our blowjobs
so he could donate blood. But he worked at a grocery store
and even with his discount, spent a day of wages

to swaddle me roses in pink, polka-dotted foil.
Some days (before you), drunk, we still traded

flirty emojis. This year I had a crisis and believed
I could pick up running. I've yet to beat
a 10-minute mile, but I can tell you where to find

the shade and jasmine, the clever, stubborn neighbor
growing her roses. I never smelled so intently,

so gratefully, until I was desperate for breath.
At my friends' funerals this year, no one wanted flowers,
but I bought them for their moms anyways. I know,

it was more for me than them. Once I bought
my mom a bouquet of lilies and she laughed

so hard I almost snatched them back.
She said, *No one ever gave me flowers!* through tears that surprised
us both. I know lilies mean death, and maybe so did she

and definitely so do you. Is that OK? A version of me
says we're going to die, so why bother leaving the warm bed?

Another says we're going to die, so let's get to the kissing.
Let the anxiety find me on the porch with the mosquitos. The shit
decaf I bought on sale? I want it if your hands boil the water.

My Boyfriend, Who Doesn't Remember Faces

My face, everyone's face, is clear and still, the surface of a pond. He only knows green, can recall every shard of olive in a stained-glass window, every teal traffic light we've sailed right through. I want our world to be a constant hue of jasmine, so each new spring bud morning, I try to make myself greener for him, greener than any Pantone swatch. I build our house from palm fronds so he knows the way home. I balance a plate of avocados on my head at cocktail parties. I stitch together shirts of guava skins for every family picnic. My cologne is muddled magnolia leaves, shredded dollar bills. Some days I'm just a stalk of celery. But even then, he pretends to mistake someone else for me, a pair of sea foam eyes for the mold I let grow in my beard. He traces the lines in their hands until I can't take any more and blow dark camo smoke out my ears. He waits until I'm a big storm of jade and fury and only then does he pull me close, only then does he say, *There you are, my little cactus—did you find the sun today?*

Hippocampus

From Greek,

sea monster

(*sic* see monster)

In my mother's

tongue *I remember*

trans: *I miss*

My tongue pared

lemon rind

scorched

in sugar

First peat

then trenchant

then copper

then plosive

then whimper

then

then

then

A Patient's Family Asks What Do I Know

In the ICU, my friend washes another friend's
face with the serum and cream samples

they hoarded from Sephora. Nurses envy
his clean, virgin skin. Saintly, as if,

a week into our friendship, he hadn't flexed
his mouth into a perfect O, ringed three fingers

around an imaginary dick to teach me the way
of efficient blowjobs. He made himself sick

on expensive gummies. He wouldn't listen
to me complain about a designer pencil case

I couldn't afford. *If you want it,*
        then want it. My gorgeous

boys and I left each other notes
with addresses of men we met online

just in case. Stuffed ourselves
into brushed out wigs just to heat up

nachos in the microwave.
               When I die

I know my loves will be dragged
up in sequins and blush, will cut the cake

with their contour. In the ICU,
my patient's mom strokes his cheekbone

while he sleeps. *You should have known him*
before this. She means before this but after

he returned to her after years of absence.
Of course my loves and I held secrets

from each other—what kind of family would we be
if we didn't gift each other the space

to learn hunger and feast in our own language?
I don't know enough of anything.

I don't think as much as do, as much
as want and miss and admire. We hold each other,

his mom and I, the morning we arrive
and he is gone. There is no rush,

I want to say to her. Our handsome
boys. We will know them again and again

when we're reborn as trees joined at the trunks,
a set of summer winds on the nude beach,

    a handful of hard candies
    melted into rainbow.

Angier, NC

I read about the winner
of the Harris Teeter gift card
and thought they lived in *Angrier*,
North Carolina. A mistake
small enough to slip into your pocket
in the checkout line.
            But I admit I'm angry.
Four of my friends died this year.
I would have more save-
the-dates for wakes than weddings
on my refrigerator door
if 30-somethings did that.
You maybe see now
why I am angry
            my friend said he was scared
to die alone and I said he was silly
instead of, *Let's get married then!*
I admit my fist has tightened
around my steering wheel
as if to say I'm ok if I'm not
screaming, as if to say look
at all the control I have.
            I admit I'm so angry that I cry
at surprise proposals now.
I'm so angry I write down
everyone's birthday.
So angry I demand unending hugs.
I'm lousy and bloated
with love. In anger I apologize
for not congratulating you sooner,
Lisa M. of Angier, North Carolina.
I'm angry and I wish you the bounty
of double coupon day, of dented cans
sold for cheap. A slab of bloody roast
with the most perfect marble.
A flat of strawberries near spoil,
right when they're sweetest.

Notes

"A Patient's Family Asks What Do I Know" is for Jamie Tam.

"Apologies to My Beloved" is after Jessica Jacobs's "A Question to Ask Once the Honeymoon is Over."

"My Father Worries War is Coming" interpolates a line from "Station," by Maria Hummel.

"Scenes (How's a Man)" owes a debt to the film *Moonlight*.

"Scenes (Does He Speak)" owes a debt to the film *Call Me by Your Name*.

"Starting with a Line by Frank Ocean Interviewing Timothee Chalamet" also appears in the anthology *Dream of the River* (Jacar Press) and references *VMAN* issue 39.

"Suboxone" interpolates a lyric from "Anthem," by Leonard Cohen.

Several poems first appear in the chapbook *Revisions* (Sibling Rivalry Press).

The sonnets in crown source their titles from approaches to and challenges in treating opiate use disorder.

Acknowledgments

Thank you to the editorial staff of the following journals, who have published earlier versions of these poems:

32 Poems — Call the Mouth and Starting with a Line by Frank Ocean Interviewing Timothee Chalamet

Adroit — How My Mother Named Me

Aquifer: Florida Review Online — Cadaver Lab and A Patient's Family Asks What Do I Know

ANMLY — Portraits of Handwashing

Bayou — Burnout

Beloit Poetry Journal — Baclofen and Catapres

Birdcoat Quarterly — My Father Worries War is Coming (He Practiced Nonviolence) and Papaver Somniferum

BODY — Double Depression

The Boiler — 10 Responses to a Clickbait Headline

Black Warrior Review — If Asked

Diagram — My Dearest Resident Brian

Bodega — Poem with Underwear and Ghost

Dialogist — The First X-Ray, featured in *Best of the Net 2015*

Diode — Aubade with Withdrawal and Naloxone

Freshwater Review — Ouroboros

Friction — Hell of a Time, Great Pretender, My Father Worries War is Coming (I Tell Him I'm Dating a Man)

Gertrude — Commuting by the Confederate Flag on I-40

Glass Poetry Journal — Scenes (Does He Speak)

Hobart — Frequent Utilizer Protocol

Juked — Pre-Coda

Missouri Review Poem of the Week — Angier, NC

One Pause Poetry — My Boyfriend, Who Doesn't Remember Faces

The Pinch — On the Psychotic Unit

Pittsburgh Poetry Journal — Bottoms

Pleiades — Ode to Bossy Bottoms

Poetry Northwest — Explaining Psychiatry to My ESL Relatives and Trust Metaphor

Rhino Poetry — Hippocampus

Salamander — Intervention

Seneca Review — Lexapro

Shade Literary Journal — Scenes (How's a Man)

Superstition Review — Untitled (Portrait of Ross in L.A.): Mixed Material: Felix Gozalez-Torres: 1991

Tupelo Quaterly — Bentyl and Nocturne

Up the Staircase — Detox

Zone 3 — Tramadol

Gratitude to the editorial staff at Diode Editions for shepherding this book, even as I stumbled along behind it. The same to the great hearts and minds at Autumn House Press, Sibling Rivalry Press, and Backbone Press. Thank you to Brandon Amico for his generosity and faith in this book — I would not have made these final steps without you.

Thank you especially to the professors, instructors, administrators, reading series coordinators, interview editors, and review writers who held my work in their hands and minds and helped me believe again and again that poetry is so important.

Thank you, as well, to my friends and family. To the Traveler's Club— Regina DiPerna, Nathan Johnson, Whitney Lawson, Anna Sutton, Gabriella Tallmadge—there will never be sufficient books and acknowledgment pages to express my love for you (so let's hope there's many more books to come!). Erik Donhowe and Jamie Tam, I'd cross the country again and again to see you. Zach Brin, McKinley Clabaugh, Amelia Cline, Emily Peele, I know love is possible. Thank you to Andrew Boylan for it all.

Finally, I've only told one clinical supervisor about the events that occurred in some of these poems. He closed his door behind me, sat, and listened. I hope we all meet or become someone like him.

Eric Tran is a queer Vietnamese poet. His debut book of poetry *The Gutter Spread Guide to Prayer* won the Autumn House Press Rising Writer Prize and was featured in *The Rumpus* Poetry Book Club and the Asian American Journalists Association–New York book club. He serves as poetry editor for Orison Books and a poetry reader for the *Los Angeles Review*. He has received awards and recognition from *Prairie Schooner, New Delta Review, Best of the Net*, and others. His work appears in *RHINO, 32 Poems*, the *Missouri Review* and elsewhere. He completed his MFA at the University of North Carolina Wilmington and is a resident physician in psychiatry in Asheville, NC.